Contents

Some words are shown in bold, **like this.** You can find out what they mean by looking in the glossary.

Chapter 1: Three great kingdoms

Between 700 and 1590 three great West African kingdoms grew just south of the Sahara Desert. Ghana came first, then Mali, and finally Songhai. They were the wealthiest, most powerful kingdoms of the region. These three kingdoms had beautiful cities, successful trade, skilled craftspeople, and strong armies.

This ceremonial sword is made from iron by skilled craftspeople.

Timeline

700 The Soninke establish Kingdom of Ghana	**1235** Kingdom of Mali forms by conquering Ghana	**1235–255** Sundjata Keita rules Mali	**1312** Mansa Musa rules Mali

Ghana

In 700 the Soninke people formed the kingdom of Ghana. They were the first in the area to use iron. The Soninke defeated their enemies with iron-tipped spears. These weapons were superior to the bone, wood, or stone weapons used by their enemies.

Ghana was located between the beginnings of the Senegal and Niger rivers. It grew to be as large as France. The capital city of Kumbi Saleh was in the centre of the country. However, poor roads made it difficult to move goods or send messages. As a result, Ghana's kings appointed princes to govern areas of the kingdom that were far from Kumbi Saleh. These princes were paid well so they stayed loyal to the king.

New nations, old names

The first name for the Kingdom of Ghana was Wagadu. It later became Ghana, meaning "war chief". This name was chosen to honour the kingdom's army leaders. In 1957, a nation named Ghana formed in western Africa. This new nation was hundreds of kilometres south of the ancient Kingdom of Ghana. It was named Ghana to honour West Africa's first important kingdom. The modern-day country of Mali is located in the same area as the ancient kingdom of Ghana.

1337 Kingdom of Songhai forms after conquering Mali

1440 Kingdom of Benin starts its rise to power

1464–1492 Sunni Ali rules Songhai

1476 Songhai captures city of Djenne

1591 Songhai conquered by Moroccans

Gold and salt passed through Ghana on trade routes. The government taxed the traders. This made the kingdom very rich. Ghana used camel **caravans** to carry out its own trade. The caravans carried goods between Ghana and other places such as Europe, Egypt, Arabia, and coastal cities of North Africa.

Ghana's wealth, strong army, and well-run government allowed it to last more than 500 years. However, in 1076, invaders won a major victory over Ghana. By 1240, Ghana had been replaced by the kingdom of Mali.

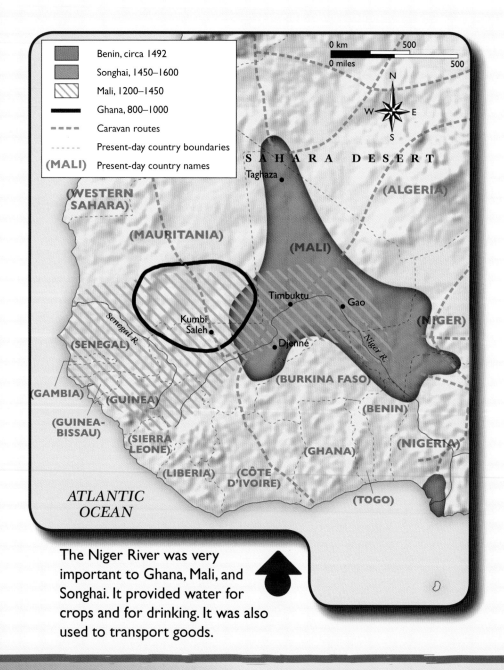

The Niger River was very important to Ghana, Mali, and Songhai. It provided water for crops and for drinking. It was also used to transport goods.

Mali

The Mandinka people lived in a fertile, southern area of Ghana. They were excellent farmers and traders. The Mandinka gained control of large parts of the Senegal and Niger rivers, as well as lands near by. A great Mandinka leader named Sundjata Keita came to power in 1235. He established the kingdom of Mali, which replaced Ghana. At first it had the same borders as Ghana, but Mali eventually spread so it had twice as much land. In 1312, Mali's greatest king, Mansa Musa, became the ruler. He increased trade and improved schools and courts. He also wanted people to adopt **Islam** as their religion. Timbuktu and Gao became the kingdom's most important cities.

The Lion King

According to some historic accounts, Sundjata Keita could not walk or talk very well when he was young. People doubted that he could ever be a leader. Somehow, though, he overcame these problems. He became so strong and successful as an army leader that he was nicknamed "The Lion King". Sundjata was also well known as a magician and mystic.

Caravans sometimes had more than 1,000 camels carrying goods to be traded. They went to markets in the cities or to orther areas where goods were exchanged with merchant ships.

Songhai

After Mansa Musa died in 1337, a group called the Songhai seized most of Mali. The Songhai people were from eastern Mali and were led by two military leaders. In 1464, one of these leaders, named Sunni Ali, became King of Songhai.

The Kingdom of Songhai was the largest and most prosperous of all the West African kingdoms. It spread more than 1,600 kilometres from what is now Niger in the east, to the Atlantic coast in the west. Its capital city was Goa. Trade grew and included goods from all over North Africa, Europe, and more distant places.

Another high-ranking army leader known as Askia Muhammad ruled from 1493 until 1528. He organized the government very well. Muhammad divided the work of the kingdom among several able helpers. In many ways Songhai's government worked in a similar way to a government in a modern nation. King Muhammad also wanted more people to accept **Islam** as their religion.

Mansa Musa once made a religious journey to Mecca. He donated much gold to people along the way.

In the 1580s, some of Songhai's people began to fight against the government leaders. This weakened the kingdom. Then in 1591, Moroccans from the north attacked. Their guns defeated Songhai's army, which still used spears. By the end of 1591 the Kingdom of Songhai broke up.

Timbuktu was once a great city of West Africa. Lack of a good water supply has made it much less important in the modern world.

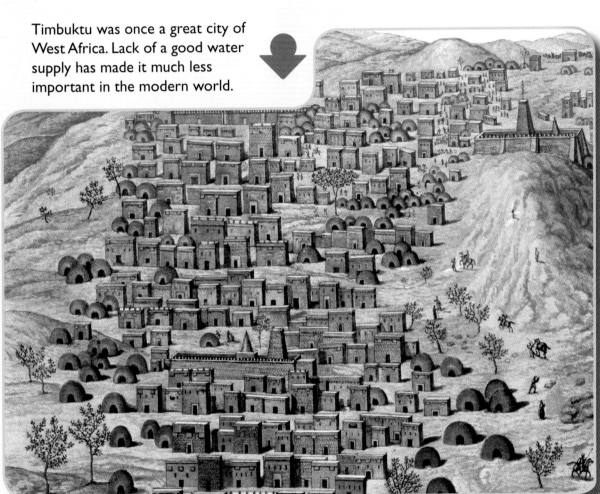

Profitable books

In 1510, a Muslim writer named Leo Africanus travelled to Timbuktu in the Kingdom of Songhai. He was pleased to see how important education was: "There are many judges, teachers, and holy men, all being greatly helped by the king, who holds students in much honour ... More money is made from selling books in Timbuktu than any other trade."

Chapter 2: Life in the kingdoms

Most people in the ancient West African kingdoms were farmers. Lack of rainfall was their main problem. The best farms were located near rivers. Rice and other grains were grown, as well as fruits and vegetables. Some food was bought from traders.

The West African kingdoms also had cities as great as any found in Europe at the time. Timbuktu, Kumbi Saleh, Djenne, and Gao were all large cities with rich societies.

The Great **Mosque** in the city of Djenne shows the building skills of West Africans. Wooden stakes can be seen sticking out from the mud walls. The stakes helped to strengthen the walls.

Families and clans

Families were important in the West African kingdoms. The father was the decision-maker, but the advice of his wife was respected. Uncles, especially the brothers of the father, played important roles.

This sculpture shows a proud mother holding her babies. Notice the neck-rings the mother wears – a popular fashion.

Boys stayed with their mothers for 12 years. After that they trained in a skill with an uncle. Wealthy boys were sent to school. Girls did not usually go to school. They were trained by their mothers in household skills until they married. They usually married by the age of 14.

Groups of families formed clans. In some villages there was only one clan. It acted like a small government. Clans often had different beliefs and habits. They did not want to join with other clans.

On the other hand...

The left hand was considered the "unclean" one. This was because there was little water for washing hands. People wanted to keep their right hand as clean as possible to use it for eating. They used their left hand for dirty tasks. This practice is still common today in some West African and Arabian areas.

Business and trade

Good trade brought wealth and changes to the kingdoms of West Africa. In the 1200s Arab traders brought new building styles. Square homes replaced round huts. The houses were made of dried mud with logs in the walls to strengthen them. In the centre of houses, there was a small open space with no roof. Food was cooked here over fires.

This is an example of West African metalwork. The culture that produced this work is descended from West African kingdoms.

The kingdoms' business systems gradually improved. **Caravans** had armed guards. Merchants had such good business skills that they could pay the high costs of moving goods and still make money. Laws were passed to make sure craftspeople provided well-made goods at fair prices. In Timbuktu and other cities of the Kingdoms, customers could also buy local goods. These included pottery, cloth, jewellry, leather, and metal goods.

Most people believed metalworkers had magical powers to change metals into useful and beautiful objects. In some towns they were treated almost like kings.

This is a magic medicine object from the Kingdom of Benin. Many West African doctors used scientific methods, but objects like these were used by medicine men.

Medicine

Timbuktu and other cities of the kingdoms were noted for their doctors. Medicine was so advanced that doctors could perform eye surgery 1,000 years ago! They realized that the mosquito caused many diseases. Doctors knew how to **vaccinate** patients so they would not catch certain diseases. This is surprising when compared to methods used by Europeans at the time. Sickness killed millions in Europe while doctors there struggled to find cures.

Clothing

Clothing was light and loose-fitting so air could flow through and keep people cool. Men wore long, light robes and sometimes head scarves or turbans as headdresses. Sometimes fabric was drawn across their faces to protect them from blowing sand.

Women wore similar clothes to men, but their clothing was more colourful and decorative. Women and men occasionally wore a long piece of fabric that extended from their waist to their ankles. Women sometimes carried infants in a cloth that was folded a bit like a backpack.

In addition to their duties in the home, ancient West African women often helped their husbands with work – farming or working at city jobs. Many still do today.

Food

Typical foods included vegetables, fruits, bread, garlic, milk, fish, chicken, and goat meat. The baobob tree was very useful. Water was collected from hollows in its trunk. Leaves were made into sauces, and were also used to make medicines. Pods called monkey bread contained seeds that were eaten and also made into drinks. The empty pods were used as cups or bowls. Food became scarce during long dry spells called droughts.

The Benin Kingdom

The Benin Kingdom began to form in the 1100s and 1200s. It was located in the modern-day country of Nigeria. The kingdom became successful in the 1400s when it began trading with the Portuguese. The kingdom lasted until the British conquered it in 1897. Today, descendants of the Benin rulers are powerful once again in Nigeria. The kingdom made beautiful bronze sculptures. Many of these sculptures are now in England. Nigeria is trying to get them returned.

Look at the headdress on this sculpture from Benin. The lines of the woven shapes fit exactly.

Chapter 3: Stories and games

Before written language was used, stories were very important. In the evening older members of a family would share funny, historic, and family tales. The stories they told taught lessons about life. They also passed down history to young people. Storytellers often acted the tales out. They wore masks and costumes. Sometimes musicians played to add to the excitement of the storytelling.

Some storytellers were also *griots*. *Griots* were hired to remember important information. A *griot* might memorize historic events and then pass the information on to others so that it could be saved without writing. Kings hired *griots* to listen to other speakers to make sure what they said was correct.

A storyteller uses hand gestures to tell a tale. Today, people in West Africa still practice traditional forms of storytelling.

People of the West African kingdoms made musical instruments from gourds, like these being used in modern-day Mali.

Mancala, which is still played today, was a popular board game. Game pieces were moved about a board and tried to capture each other. If no board was available, people played it on the ground with stones for game pieces. Children had simple toys made from wood and other objects. Muscial instruments were made from dried gourds, wood, strings, and leather.

By doing the hands-on activities and crafts in this chapter, you will get a feel for what life was like in the West African Kingdoms.

Recipe: Benne cakes

Because of dry conditions and poor soil, West Africans had to make use of every possible food. Plant seeds that could not otherwise be used sometimes became important foodstuffs. The recipe here uses sesame seeds, but other types of seeds such as monkey bread (part of a baobab tree), and pumpkin seeds were used too. *Bennes* means "sesame seeds" in Malinke languages. The Malinke people are spread throughout West Africa.

Warning!

An adult should always be present when you are using a hot oven.

Read all directions before beginning the recipe.

Supplies and ingredients
- oil or butter for greasing tray
- 250 g firmly-packed brown sugar
- 50 g butter or margarine, softened
- 1 egg, beaten
- ½ teaspoon vanilla extract
- 1 teaspoon lemon juice
- 65 g plain flour
- ½ teaspoon baking powder
- ¼ teaspoon salt
- 250 g toasted sesame seeds
- baking tray

Sesame seeds are smaller than rice. They have little taste unless they are toasted or mixed with other foods.

1. Preheat the oven to 170° C.

2. Lightly grease the baking tray. You can use the wrapper from the butter to do this, or a paper towel with a small amount of oil on it.

3. Mix the brown sugar and butter and beat until they are creamy.

4. Stir in the egg, vanilla extract, and lemon juice.

5. Add the flour, baking powder, salt, and sesame seeds. Mix well.

6. Drop rounded teaspoons of the mix on to the baking tray, about 5 centimetres apart.

7. Bake for 15 minutes, or until the edges are brown.

Benne cakes

The recipe for *benne* cakes was brought to the United States by West African slaves. Today, some African Americans make these treats for holiday celebrations such as Kwanzaa.

Activity: Make a mask

Traditional West Africans believed in the power of magic and of spirits. Masks were a way to communicate with spirits. The mask you make will be made of paper products, but masks in the kingdoms were made of wood or metal.

Warning!
Read all directions before beginning the project.

Supplies

- strong paper plate
- thin cardboard, stiff coloured card, or thick paper that can be cut with scissors.
- masking tape
- plaster gauze strips – about 500 g per mask, and a water cup
- scissors
- pencil
- paint and brush
- about one metre of ribbon or wool
- fabric or hot glue (optional)
- crepe paper, tissue paper, shells, beads, seeds, foil, leather, other decorations (optional)

Different types of masks had different meanings. Some were a sign of human qualities, such as power or wisdom, while others represented animals or some well-known character.

1 The paper plate will form the main face area of the mask. What kind of mask will you make? Will it be an animal? Will it be a supernatural mask?

2 Write your name on the inside of the plate. Look at your name, and hold the the plate upright in front of your nose. Carefully place your fingers where you believe your eyes holes should be made.

3 Put the plate upside down on your work surface. Use a pencil to poke holes where you think the eyes should be. Keep the holes as small as you can. (See Picture A)

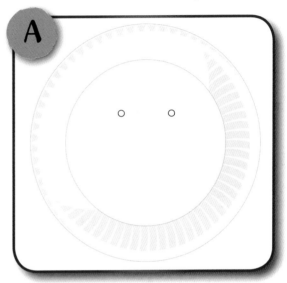

4 Put the plate back in front of your face. Make sure the eye-holes are in the right place. Don't worry if you have to try making eyes again; the extra holes will be covered later. When you have them in the right place, use scissors to enlarge the holes so you can easily see through the mask.

5 Use the same process to cut holes for your mouth and nose, if you think they are necessary.

6 Use a pencil or a hole-punch to make two holes near the edge of the mask – one on the left edge and one on the right. This is where you will attach the loops that hold the mask on to your face. (See Picture B)

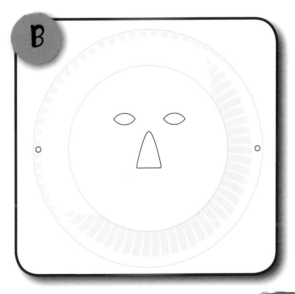

7 Think about what other facial features you need to add, such as ears, eyebrows, snout or nose, mouth, teeth, scales, etc. Draw these parts on the cardboard or coloured card, and cut them out. (Hint: if you draw near the edge of the cardboard, you will have less to cut.) Tape these features onto the plate. (See Picture C)

8 When your mask has all its basic features, use plaster gauze to cover it. Make sure the strips are about 2.5 cm by 7.5 cm. Dip them into the water cup one piece at a time. When you take them out of the water, squeeze the extra water out between two fingers, and lay the plaster gauze on your mask. (See Picture D)

9 Repeat this process, placing each piece of gauze beside the last strip. Cover the entire mask and all the cardboard features. Don't cover the eyes or any other openings that you want to keep open.

10 Cover the entire mask with three layers of plaster gauze. To make it extra strong, arrrange the strips on the second layer so they criss-cross the strips on the first layer. Then criss-cross again for the third layer. Be sure to secure all of the cardboard features with the plaster – the tape is only temporary until the plaster dries. (See Picture E)

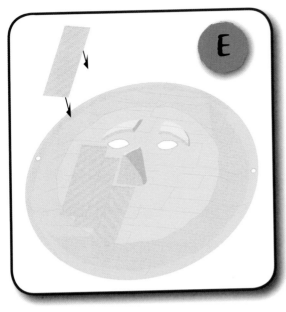

E

⑪ Let the mask dry overnight. You will know which one is yours because it will have your name on the inside.

⑫ Once the mask is dry, you can outline the details with a pencil, and then paint them. You can also add decorations, such as beads, shells, or other items that would be appropriate for your mask.

⑬ Cut two pieces of ribbon or wool, each about 45 centimetres long. Run one piece through one of the holes on the side edge of the mask, and tie it there. Repeat this process with the hole on the other side, tying some ribbon or wool there. Tie the ribbon or wool together behind your head to wear the mask.

Mask

Your mask will look similar to this when it is finished.

Will you use your mask for a particular ceremony of function? How does the design reflect this?

Activity: Playing mancala

Mancala may be the world's oldest board game. West Africans began playing it more than 1,000 years ago and it is still played today. It can be played anywhere by drawing a game board on the ground.

Warning!

Read all directions before beginning the project.

If you are using permanent paint, make sure you protect your workspace and your clothing.

Supplies

- 1 cardboard egg carton from a dozen eggs (or two 6-egg cartons)
- 2 clean, short tins with tops removed (such as tuna or cat food tins), or similar containers (baby food jars, small food containers, etc.)
- paint and brush (Note: If the containers do not have paper labels, poster paint will not stick to them. Use a permanent paint like acrylics or other craft paint to apply directly to metal, glass, or plastic.)
- 48 marbles, small stones, beans, or other small playing pieces

This shows a real *mancala* board and items that are used as game pieces.

1. Paint the egg carton.

2. Paint the tins or containers. These will be the *mancalas* for each player. Once again, decide how you will paint them.

Mancalas and board

How will you paint your mancalas so that you can tell them apart for each player?

How to play

- **Number of players:** 2
- **Object:** to collect the most marbles before one of the players clears their side of the egg carton of all its marbles.
- **Setting up the game:** The egg carton goes lengthwise between the two players. The egg carton cups closest to each player make up their side of the board. Each player places a *mancala* to his or her right. They place 4 marbles in each of the cups in the egg carton playing board: 48 in all.

PLAYING:
- The first player picks up all 4 of the marbles from any one of the cups on the board.
- Starting with the next cup to the right, he puts one marble in each of the next four cups. If he reaches the end of his side of the board, he can place a marble in the second player's *mancala,* then continue placing marbles in his opponent's cups. If his last marble goes in the other player's *mancala*, he gets another turn. Where on the board should he start to make sure this happens?
- If the player drops his last marble on his own side, and if that cup was empty, the player captures all the marbles in his opponent's cup directly across from the empty one.
- All the captured marbles, including the capturing marble, go into the player's *mancala*.
- The game ends when one of the players has no marbles left in the cups on their side of the playing board. Count the marbles in each mancala: the player with the most marbles wins.

25

Activity: Make a kente cloth

A kente cloth is a narrow strip of material that circles a person's body. It hangs from one shoulder and extends diagonally to the waist. In the West African kingdoms, kings and very important people first wore them to impress others. Colours and shapes on the cloth stood for family names, qualities of people, and other things the wearer wanted people to know.

Warning!

This activity begins as a group project.

Read all the directions before gathering supplies and beginning.

Today, many African nations are trying to modernize, but they also want to preserve important traditions. In Africa, kente cloths are sometimes worn over modern clothes.

Supplies

- At least 7.5 metres of white 1-metre wide lining or craft paper and room to unroll it. If this is not possible, cut 1-metre sections and place each section on a different workspace.
- another length of 1-metre-wide lining paper, about 1.5 to 2 metres long. (optional)
- pencils
- paint and brushes, sponges, or other painting tools for everyone
- thin card or heavy paper, cut to about 30 cm by 30 cm per person (optional)
- long measuring sticks
- scissors
- glue
- wool or markers (optional)

1 Use a pencil and the measuring stick to divide the long roll of paper into six sections running lengthwise. Groups of people can work together to do this. Each section should be 30 centimetres wide, and run the whole length of the paper.

2 Cut the paper into long strips along the pencil lines.

3 Use a pencil to very lightly label each section with a different colour. Traditional colours include red (symbolizing life or blood,) blue (innocence,) green (earth), and gold (strength and fortune). (See Picture A)

A

1m

30cm

30cm

30cm

30cm

4 Work in teams to paint entire sections of the paper with the appropriate colour.

5 While the paint is still wet, use other colours to paint geometric designs, patterns, and shapes onto each section. Use different colours, but don't get carried away. The colour you see the most should still be the background colour. For instance, if you are painting on the blue section, you can use brushes or sponges to make green and purple dots, lines, and shapes, but the section should still be mainly blue.

6 When the paper is completely dry, turn it over and use the measuring stick to mark off every 30 cm. Cut the paper into 30-cm slices. (It may be easier to ask an adult to use a school paper cutter to make these cuts quickly.) (See Picture B)

B

7 Take each 30-cm square of every colour and fold it in half. Then fold it in half again.

8 Open the paper and cut along the folds. Each paper should end up being cut into 15-cm by 15-cm squares.

9 Decide if your group will make one kente cloth or each person will make his or her own. If the group is going to make one big cloth, pupils will glue pieces of the coloured paper onto the 1.5- to 2-metre piece of lining paper. If pupils are going to make their own kente cloths, they will glue pieces of the coloured paper onto their own pieces of card.

10 Decide on a theme for your kente cloth. What do you want it to represent?

⓫ When you have decided on a theme, begin to glue the appropriate colour of paper onto the thin card or lining paper. Just as when you painted the paper, you can use all the colours, but the overriding colour should match your theme colour – for example, green for earth.

⓬ When your cloth is complete, you could glue wool along the edges of the paper pieces, so that the pattern is easier to see. Or outline the pieces with permanent markers.

⓭ Be ready to explain your cloth to other people.

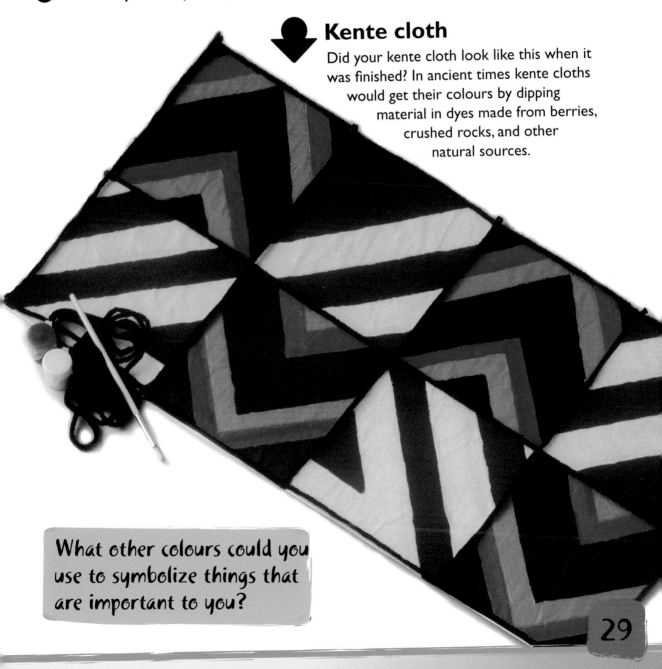

Kente cloth

Did your kente cloth look like this when it was finished? In ancient times kente cloths would get their colours by dipping material in dyes made from berries, crushed rocks, and other natural sources.

What other colours could you use to symbolize things that are important to you?

Glossary

caravans groups of traders travelling on land

Islam religion based on the teachings of Muhammad

mosque a place of worship for people who follow Islam

vaccinate inject a virus into a body to prevent catching a disease

More books to read

All About Continents: Africa, Europe and Asia, Bruce McClish (Heinemann Library, 2004)

Mansa Musa: The lion of Mali, Khephra Burns (Gulliver Books, 2001)

The instructions for the crafts and activities are designed to allow pupils to work as independently as possible. However, it is always a good idea to make a prototype before assigning any project so that pupils can see how their own work will look when completed. Prior to introducing these activities, teachers should collect and prepare the materials and be ready for any modifications that may be necessary. Participating in the project-making process will help teachers understand the directions and be ready to assist pupils with difficult steps. Teachers might also choose to adapt or modify the projects to better suit the needs of an individual child or class. No one knows the levels of achievement pupils will reach better than their teacher.

While it is preferable for pupils to work as independently as possible, there is some flexibility in regards to project materials and tools. They can vary according to what is available. For instance, while standard white glue may be most familiar, there might be times when a teacher will choose to speed up a project by using a hot glue gun to join materials. Where plaster gauze is not availabe, papier mâché can often be used. Likewise, while a project may call for leather cord, in most instances it is possible to substitute plastic rope or even wool or string. Acrylic paint may be recommended because it adheres better to a material like felt or plastic, but other types of paint would be suitable as well. Circles can be drawn with a compass, or simply by tracing a cup, roll of tape, or other circular object. Allowing pupils a broad spectrum of creativity and opportunities to problem-solve within the parameters of a given project will encourage their critical thinking skills most fully.

Each project contains a question within the directions. These questions are meant to be thought-provoking and promote discussion while pupils work on the project.

Index